FRANCIS FRITH'S

CROYDON LIVING MEMORIES

THE FRANCIS FRITH COLLECTION

www.francisfrith.com

Francis Frith's

Croydon
Living Memories

Photographic Memories

Francis Frith's
Croydon Living Memories

Martin Andrew

First published in the United Kingdom in 2000 by
The Francis Frith Collection®

Hardback Edition 2002
ISBN 1-85937-579-0

Paperback Edition 2000
ISBN 1-85937-162-0

Reprinted in Paperback 2002, 2006

British Library Cataloguing in Publication Data

Croydon Living Memories
Martin Andrew
ISBN 1-85937-162-0

The Francis Frith Collection®
Frith's Barn, Teffont,
Salisbury, Wiltshire SP3 5QP
Tel: +44 (0) 1722 716 376
Email: info@francisfrith.co.uk
www.francisfrith.com

Printed and bound in Great Britain

Front Cover: Croydon, North End c1955 C201086t

The colour-tinting is for illustrative purposes only, and is not intended to be historically accurate

Contents

Francis Frith: *Victorian Pioneer*

FRANCIS FRITH, Victorian founder of the world-famous photographic archive, was a complex and multitudinous man. A devout Quaker and a highly successful Victorian businessman, he was both philosophic by nature and pioneering in outlook.

By 1855 Francis Frith had already established a wholesale grocery business in Liverpool, and sold it for the astonishing sum of £200,000, which is the equivalent today of over £15,000,000. Now a very rich man, he was able to indulge his passion for travel. As a child he had pored over travel books written by early explorers, and his fancy and imagination had been stirred by family holidays to the sublime mountain regions of Wales and Scotland. 'What a land of spirit-stirring and enriching scenes and places!' he had written. He was to return to these scenes of grandeur in later years to 'recapture the thousands of vivid and tender memories', but with a different purpose. Now in his thirties, and captivated by the new science of photography, Frith set out on a series of pioneering journeys to the Nile regions that occupied him from 1856 until 1860.

Intrigue and Adventure

He took with him on his travels a specially-designed wicker carriage that acted as both dark-room and sleeping chamber. These far-flung journeys were packed with intrigue and adventure. In his life story, written when he was sixty-three, Frith tells of being held captive by bandits, and of fighting 'an awful midnight battle to the very point of surrender with a deadly pack of hungry, wild dogs'. Sporting flowing Arab costume, Frith arrived at Akaba by camel sixty years before Lawrence, where he encountered 'desert princes and rival sheikhs, blazing with jewel-hilted swords'.

During these extraordinary adventures he was assiduously exploring the desert regions bordering the Nile and patiently recording the antiquities and peoples with his camera. He was the first photographer to venture beyond the sixth cataract. Africa was still the mysterious 'Dark Continent', and Stanley and Livingstone's historic meeting was a decade into the future. The conditions for picture taking confound belief. He laboured for hours in his wicker dark-room in the sweltering heat of the desert, while the volatile chemicals fizzed dangerously in their trays. Often he was forced to work in remote tombs and caves where conditions were cooler. Back in London he exhibited his photographs and was 'rapturously cheered' by members of the Royal Society. His reputation as a photographer was made overnight. An eminent modern historian has likened their impact on the population of the time to that on our own generation of the first photographs taken on the surface of the moon.

Venture of a Life-Time

Characteristically, Frith quickly spotted the opportunity to create a new business as a specialist publisher of photographs. He lived in an era of immense and sometimes violent change. For the poor in the early part of Victoria's reign work was a drudge and the hours long, and people had precious little free time to enjoy themselves. Most had no transport other than a cart or gig at their disposal, and had not travelled far beyond

the boundaries of their own town or village. However, by the 1870s, the railways had threaded their way across the country, and Bank Holidays and half-day Saturdays had been made obligatory by Act of Parliament. All of a sudden the ordinary working man and his family were able to enjoy days out and see a little more of the world.

With characteristic business acumen, Francis Frith foresaw that these new tourists would enjoy having souvenirs to commemorate their days out. In 1860 he married Mary Ann Rosling and set out with the intention of photographing every city, town and village in Britain. For the next thirty years he travelled the country by train and by pony and trap, producing fine photographs of seaside resorts and beauty spots that were keenly bought by millions of Victorians. These prints were painstakingly pasted into family albums and pored over during the dark nights of winter, rekindling precious memories of summer excursions.

The Rise of Frith & Co

Frith's studio was soon supplying retail shops all over the country. To meet the demand he gathered about him a small team of photographers, and published the work of independent artist-photographers of the calibre of Roger Fenton and Francis Bedford. In order to gain some understanding of the scale of Frith's business one only has to look at the catalogue issued by Frith & Co in 1886: it runs to some 670 pages, listing not only many thousands of views of the British Isles but also many photographs of most European countries, and China, Japan, the USA and

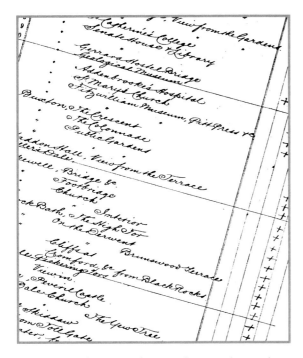

Canada – note the sample page shown above from the hand-written *Frith & Co* ledgers detailing pictures taken. By 1890 Frith had created the greatest specialist photographic publishing company in the world, with over 2,000 outlets – more than the combined number that Boots and W H Smith have today! The picture on the right shows the *Frith & Co* display board at Ingleton in the Yorkshire Dales (left of window). Beautifully constructed with a mahogany frame and gilt inserts, it could display up to a dozen local scenes.

Postcard Bonanza

The ever-popular holiday postcard we know today took many years to develop. In 1870 the Post Office issued the first plain cards, with a pre-printed stamp on one face. In 1894 they allowed other publishers' cards to be sent through the mail with an attached adhesive halfpenny stamp. Demand grew rapidly, and

in 1895 a new size of postcard was permitted called the court card, but there was little room for illustration. In 1899, a year after Frith's death, a new card measuring 5.5 x 3.5 inches became the standard format, but it was not until 1902 that the divided back came into being, with address and message on one face and a full-size illustration on the other. *Frith & Co* were in the vanguard of postcard development, and Frith's sons Eustace and Cyril continued their father's monumental task, expanding the number of views offered to the public and recording more and more places in Britain, as the coasts and countryside were opened up to mass travel.

Francis Frith died in 1898 at his villa in Cannes, his great project still growing. The archive he created continued in business for another seventy years. By 1970 it contained over a third of a million pictures of 7,000 cities, towns and villages. The massive photographic record Frith has left to us stands as a living monument to a special and very remarkable man.

Frith's Archive: *A Unique Legacy*

FRANCIS FRITH'S legacy to us today is of immense significance and value, for the magnificent archive of evocative photographs he created provides a unique record of change in 7,000 cities, towns and villages throughout Britain over a century and more. Frith and his fellow studio photographers revisited locations many times down the years to update their views, compiling for us an enthralling and colourful pageant of British life and character.

We tend to think of Frith's sepia views of Britain as nostalgic, for most of us use them to conjure up memories of places in our own lives with which we have family associations. It often makes us forget that to Francis Frith they were records of daily life as it was actually being lived in the cities, towns and villages of his day. The Victorian age was one of great and often bewildering change for ordinary people,

and though the pictures evoke an impression of slower times, life was as busy and hectic as it is today.

We are fortunate that Frith was a photographer of the people, dedicated to recording the minutiae of everyday life. For it is this sheer wealth of visual data, the painstaking chronicle of changes in dress, transport, street layouts, buildings, housing, engineering and landscape that captivates us so much today. His remarkable images offer us a powerful link with the past and with the lives of our ancestors.

Today's Technology

Computers have now made it possible for Frith's many thousands of images to be accessed almost instantly. In the Frith archive today, each photograph is carefully 'digitised' then stored on a CD Rom. Frith archivists can locate a single photograph amongst thousands within seconds. Views can be catalogued and sorted under a variety of categories of place and content to the immediate benefit of researchers.

Inexpensive reference prints can be created for them at the touch of a mouse button, and a wide range of books and other printed materials assembled and published for a wider, more general readership - in the next twelve months over a hundred Frith local history titles will be published! The day-to-day workings of the archive are very different from how they were in Francis Frith's time: imagine the herculean task of sorting through eleven tons of glass negatives as Frith had to do to locate a

See Frith at www.francisfrith.com

particular sequence of pictures! Yet the archive still prides itself on maintaining the same high standards of excellence laid down by Francis Frith, including the painstaking cataloguing and indexing of every view.

It is curious to reflect on how the internet now allows researchers in America and elsewhere greater instant access to the archive than Frith himself ever enjoyed. Many thousands of individual views can be called up on screen within seconds on one of the Frith internet sites, enabling people living continents away to revisit the streets of their ancestral home town, or view places in Britain where they have enjoyed holidays. Many overseas researchers welcome the chance to view special theme selections, such as transport, sports, costume and ancient monuments.

We are certain that Francis Frith would have heartily approved of these modern developments in imaging techniques, for he himself was always working at the very limits of Victorian photographic technology.

The Value of the Archive Today

Because of the benefits brought by the computer, Frith's images are increasingly studied by social historians, by researchers into genealogy and ancestory, by architects, town planners, and by teachers and schoolchildren involved in local history projects.

In addition, the archive offers every one of us an opportunity to examine the places where we and our families have lived and worked down the years. Highly successful in Frith's own era, the archive is now, a century and more on, entering a new phase of popularity.

The Past in Tune with the Future

Historians consider the Francis Frith Collection to be of prime national importance. It is the only archive of its kind remaining in private ownership and has been valued at a million pounds. However, this figure is now rapidly increasing as digital technology enables more and more people around the world to enjoy its benefits.

Francis Frith's archive is now housed in an historic timber barn in the beautiful village of Teffont in Wiltshire. Its founder would not recognize the archive office as it is today. In place of the many thousands of dusty boxes containing glass plate negatives and an all-pervading odour of photographic chemicals, there are now ranks of computer screens. He would be amazed to watch his images travelling round the world at unimaginable speeds through network and internet lines.

The archive's future is both bright and exciting. Francis Frith, with his unshakeable belief in making photographs available to the greatest number of people, would undoubtedly approve of what is being done today with his lifetime's work. His photographs, depicting our shared past, are now bringing pleasure and enlightenment to millions around the world a century and more after his death.

Croydon - *An Introduction*

TO MANY PEOPLE Croydon is a modern town, a forest of tall office blocks intersected by dual carriageways, fly-overs and underpasses: a town apparently redeveloped with scant regard for its history. I moved to Carshalton, three miles to the west, as a twelve-year-old boy; it was 1959, just as the redevelopment got under way. I well remember the excitement of going to my first concert in the brand new Fairfield Halls, Croydon's rival to the Royal Festival Hall, and the first sign of a cultural renaissance amid the new towers dedicated to Mammon. That is all forty years ago or so, and the wholesale rebuilding and consequent destruction of much of the centre and periphery of what had been a fine market town looks a trifle quaint now. Croydon had greatly expanded, of course, with the arrival of the railways from 1839; this gave the town some excellent Victorian architecture.

Much of this was swept away after the Croydon Corporation Act of 1956 in a programme combining new road networks, infrastucture and commercial and public buildings at the height of the era when sweeping away the old 'outdated' buildings of historic towns and cities was seen as the only path for regeneration. Croydon was not alone here: Uxbridge, for example, merrily punched its heart out; other towns, such as Plymouth and Coventry, at least had the justification of being bombed flat and having to start again. The pride of Croydon's councillors, planners, highway engineers, businessmen and virtually everyone else in what was being done is perhaps reflected in the third chapter of

this book, which shows the Frith photographers enthusiastically recording the new developments for postcard production. I find myself in the curious position of remembering the Brave New World excitement as the new buildings arose, resulting in a sort of miniature Manhattan in south London with a type of skyline we had never seen before. I was living through a remarkable phase of the town's history; now that I am involved professionally in conserving the built heritage, I have for some years swung the other way and have been somewhat scathing of the town's casting off its past in such a cavalier and thoroughgoing way. I was therefore delighted to be offered the chance to do this book. The photographs range from about 1948, when trams still ran in the town, through the mid 1950s, before the changes came, and then to the early 1960s, after the first wave had achieved what the town fathers wanted. There have been rebuildings and new buildings since, but the main historical phase of the greatest and most far-reaching changes are encompassed in this book, which, unlike most others in the Frith Photographic Memories series, covers less than twenty years.

However, despite all this change, the fundamentals of a town prove more difficult to destroy. Indeed, there are buildings of outstanding importance and historic significance that still survive, including an archbishop's medieval palace and a Tudor hospital or almshouses. The main streets of the town, a pattern established by the end of the Middle Ages, is still clearly discernible. There is a large triangular market place with the High Street forming its east side. North of this, the High Street continues as North End, and to the south, beyond Coombe Road, it continues as South End. This is the old London to Brighton road. The north side of the market place is Crown Hill, which continues west as Church Street and east as George Street. The west side of the market place is Surrey Street, where the street market still takes place. The centre of the market place has long been encroached upon in the well-known process whereby temporary market stalls are replaced by permanent buildings. To the west of the town centre is the medieval parish church and the medieval palace of the Archbishops of Canterbury, both separated by low-lying marshy ground with fish-ponds and streams and one area surrounded by streams known as Bog Island: I think you get the picture.

In 1839 the London and Croydon Railway opened, and in 1841 the London and Brighton Railway followed with East Croydon Station. Thus began the transformation of a market town that eventually led to our own day. I will now look at the evolution of Croydon up to this moment of transformation, when a town whose population had grown from about 5,750 in 1801 to 18,000 in

1841 suddenly took off and reached over 100,000 by 1891.

The town originally grew up around the parish church to the west of the present market place, and it was here that the archbishops of Canterbury built one of their palaces. The manor was held by the archbishops by the time of Domesday Book, but it was inevitable that the town's economic centre of gravity would migrate eastward to the London road, where the market place was laid out to take advantage of the commercial traffic. It was long known as a prosperous corn market. Within the Archbishop's Palace is probably a 12th-century core, but its chief glory is the Great Hall, built in the 1380s and altered in the 1440s. The rest of the medieval remains includes the Archbishop's chapel of the 1460s; the Guardroom was converted to an audience chamber in around 1400, and may incorporate the original 12th-century upper hall that preceded the present Great Hall. It is now a school and preserved, but after the Archbishops sold it in 1780 it went through difficult times and much was demolished. The medieval parish church to its north suffered a disastrous fire in 1867 and was largely rebuilt by Sir George Gilbert Scott.

Across the marshy ground up Crown Hill, the town grew to become one of a ring of corn and produce markets fringing London and supplying the capital's insatiable appetite. The Archbishops continued to take an interest in the town, none more than John Whitgift, Archbishop from 1583 to 1604; his alabaster effigy can be seen in the parish church where he was buried. He founded the almshouses, or Hospital of the Holy Trinity, at the corner of George Street, a quadrangle of brick buildings erected between 1596 and 1599, a remarkable survival in the centre of a town so keen to modernise. He also established the Whitgift School, whose Master's House, just off George Street, was demolished in 1897; it was local outrage over this that saved the Whitgift Hospital from demolition a few years later. His 1596 school foundation was revived in the 1860s, and Sir Arthur Blomfield designed Tudor-style buildings for the site off North End. The school moved to Shirley, and the buildings were demolished in 1965 (I remember it happening); their site and the 12 acres of playing fields were redeveloped for a vast covered shopping mall and - inevitably for 1960s Croydon - a tower block of offices, Rothschild House. As a genuflection to the past, this vast complex was named the Whitgift Centre. From the mid 1980s it has been entirely remodelled, modernised and partly rebuilt.

The town acquired its first Town Hall around 1566 on the west side of High Street at the southern end of the market place; it prospered into the 19th century as a trade and market

centre, with brewing and other industries. Until the mid-Victorian period, the town looked like any other market town in Surrey, with a mix of timber-framed buildings, brick Georgian and later frontages and a market place built over with rank alleys between ramshackle slums and a large population crammed into the buildings, many of whom were prostitutes and criminals. Of more pressing concern to the early Victorian townsmen was the appalling sanitation: there were rank stinking ponds, fetid waterways and frequent flooding that separated the market place from the old town. In 1848 the Public Health Act provided powers for the setting up of local health boards, and Croydon was one of the first to do so. The Board's report was no worse than for other towns of the period, such as High Wycombe in Buckinghamshire; it painted a picture of open privies discharging into water courses, rubbish and faeces thrown into public drains, tainted wells next to privies, drinking water polluted, and so on, with dense rank fogs and mists, frequent flooding, and churchyards with coffins buried one upon the other to within inches of the surface. The Board vigorously set about improving things: the streams and runnels disappeared, good drains were laid and a clean water supply provided. The health of the citizens, both rich and poor, benefited immensely. The most notable evidence of this is the old Waterworks building

behind Surrey Street. The Board bought and re-erected the West Croydon Engine House of the Croydon Atmospheric Railway, which ran from Forest Hill to West Croydon from 1845 to 1847. The date '1851' records this rebuild. The taller battlemented 'castle' was added in 1867. Further additions followed; a further element of the Board's improvements included the reservoirs and a neo-Norman water tower of 1867 erected in Coombe Cliff Gardens.

In 1883 the town became a borough, and from 1888 until 1965 was a County Borough. The second Town Hall had replaced the first in 1808, a stucco Regency building of some quality, but this made way for the present superb Town Hall on Katharine Street; it was built on the station site of a branch line that ran the short distance from East Croydon Station to the back of the High Street, which had closed in 1890. In fact, the town hall gardens preserve part of its cutting. This proud building with its tall tower is still the focus of the town; its gardens, now expanded by the inclusion of the site of the old police station and re-opened by the Queen in 1983, are a popular meeting-place and the spot where office workers eat their sandwiches.

Under the enterprising mayor Alderman Frederick Edridge, who laid the Town Hall's foundation stone in June 1892, the problem of the market slums was tackled with characteristic

vigour. The town secured the Croydon Improvement Act in 1890, which empowered compulsory purchase of properties in the triangle. The second town hall was demolished, the High Street widened and the market infill mostly demolished and rebuilt. A plaque by Milletts commemorates all this; the plaque was unveiled by Mayor Edridge in 1896. The 1890s were a boom time for rebuilding much of central Croydon, and new building continued with vigour until World War II, including the long Oxford Street-style facade of Allders, one of the town's three major department stores, in 1926. Kennards and Grants were the other two. The former was replaced by the modern Drummond Centre and a Debenhams. Grants has recently been demolished, apart from some of the superb 1890s facades on the High Street. Other important buildings included the Grand Theatre of 1896 and the Davis Theatre of 1928, a 3,700-seater. The town acquired trams, which can be seen in the earliest views in this book from the late 1940s; the trams disappeared in 1951.

After World War II, the town stagnated until the Croydon Corporation Act of 1956. This found circumstances just right for success: closeness to London with excellent rail links, lower office rentals than London, official encouragement for firms to leave London (we all remember the adverts for the delights of working in the country pushed out by the Location of Offices Bureau) and a go-ahead modernising Council. Consequently huge office blocks arose, many of paralysing mediocrity, some of considerable distinction and well-detailed. Among the latter I would include the first Norfolk House by Howell and Brookes of 1958, and perhaps Suffolk House, a four-storey building of 1960 by Raglan Squires, which employed the then-popular coloured panel below the window style. It has to be admitted, though, that most of the office blocks relentlessly interpreted their brief, which was to enclose as much space as high as possible - this approach leaves architecture trailing in the wake of rental returns. St George House, now Nestle's, is a good example of the gigantism prevalent at the time, while Leon House is a monster that destroys the integrity of the southern part of the High Street. Some of the blocks commemorate the buildings they replaced: Davis House in the High Street supplanted the Davis Theatre, while the Whitgift Centre, a vast shopping complex with an office tower, nods to the Archbishop's school which was removed to make way for it.

Amid the flyovers, underpasses and dual carriageways there are distinguished buildings: the Fairfield Halls have stood the test of time, and Croydon College has its good points, particularly facing Park Lane. Others are gross and insulting, such as BT's Ryland House. From a distance, Croydon's commercial centre rises like Dallas from the suburbs; but the interesting feature of

Croydon is that much of its Victorian and pre-World War I heritage survived the architectural onslaught, partly because the focus of the great rebuild was parallel to the old town's streets. George Street all but disappeared east of Park Lane, a flyover bisects the High Street, 1960s buildings replace older buildings on Surrey Street, and there has been much insensitive alteration and rebuilding on smaller scales too. However, there is enough left to make a visit very rewarding, and the revival of the tramway network is a most exciting development. Away from the commercial centre, small-scale houses survive, and the council, since 1965 the London Borough of Croydon, continues to improve the town. For instance, they have given partial priority to pedestrians in North End, and have encouraged the restoration of historic buildings.

I had not paid more than fleeting visits to Croydon since the late 1960s, and I was curious to see how it had evolved. I was impressed, and I greatly enjoyed my research visits; I advise overcoming any prejudices you may have. The town survives remarkably, despite the vast changes it has had to absorb since 1956, and contains buildings that in other contexts would be very well-known indeed, not secrets to Croydon people alone. At its heart, the Tudor brick of the Whitgift Hospital is in a sense a symbol of remarkable continuity in a location one would have thought highly vulnerable to the forces of progress. The buildings have seen all sorts of changes; now brand-new, silent trams glide past the Hospital once again.

Some Important Buildings, Churches and Parks

View from the Town Hall Tower c1954 C201067
The first three photographs, taken from the Town Hall tower, give a splendid view of the town before 1960s tower blocks and new roads so radically changed Croydon. Here we look west across High Street past the castle (in fact the Waterworks of 1867) to the fine tower of the parish church of St John. To its left is the large gable of one of the Archbishop of Canterbury's medieval palaces, now Old Palace School. To its right is the loading bay and yard of Page and Overton's brewery in Church Road, which closed in 1954.

◀ **View from the Town Hall Tower c1955** C201069
The last view from the Town Hall tower looks almost north along North End. The High Street is on the left, with the varied Jacobean and Dutch styles popular in the 1890s, while Grants store advertises its summer sale. Much has been lost in this view, including the church-like tower on the right, which was the centrepiece of the Whitgift School; now it and the school fields are under the huge Whitgift Shopping Centre.

View from the Town Hall Tower c1955 C201068

The second view looks north-west across the 1890s Dutch gables of High Street with the now-demolished rear block of Grants department store. Beyond the trees of Wandle Park are the cooling towers, chimneys and gasholders of Croydon Power Station. In the last twenty years the power station has been demolished except for the two chimneys to the right of the gasometers: they are now eye-catchers for an Ikea store.

Katharine Street c1955 ▶
C201074

The former town hall, a dignified stucco building of 1808 with a shallow pediment and clock cupola, stood in the High Street where the current Millet's shop is located, at the junction of Surrey Street and High Street. The Croydon Improvement Act of 1890 provided for the widening of the High Street, and the old town hall was demolished in 1893 after the new one was under way in nearby Katharine Street. At the right is the grand Union Bank of 1893, now the Spread Eagle pub.

The Town Hall c1965
C201210

Amid all the change Croydon has seen, the Town Hall has held its own as a symbol of municipal pride since its foundation stone was laid in June 1892 by the town's most enterprising and dynamic Victorian mayor, Alderman Frederick Edridge. This view looks east from high up in the Fairfield Hall past the town hall gardens.

The Town Hall c1965 C201150

The Dutch/Flemish part on the right is the public library, originally entered via the porch in front of the tower.
Beyond are the corporation offices which opened in 1895; the tower is an elegant junction between the two
elements. Part of the library is now the Clocktower museum and arts complex. The mix of red brick and Portland
stone adds to the crisp dignity of the building, recently cleaned and well restored.

The Town Hall c1955 C201058

In the foreground, in front of the lower part of the tower, is the War Memorial with figures by Montford, dated 1923, while John Whitgift sits on his chair in front of the former corn exchange. Queen Victoria's statue by Williamson, 1903, has now moved to a new location in front of the corn exchange so that new steps into the Clocktower centre could be made. On the right is the Italianate Union Bank Chambers of 1893.

The Town Hall Gardens c1950 C201011

The Town Hall and the gardens to its east were built and formed in the cutting of the branch line which ran from East Croydon Station on the London, Brighton and South Coast Railway to the back of High Street. This remarkably short branch line opened in 1866 and closed in 1890. The gardens preserve the cutting, while the Town Hall and Library basements rise from the site of the station platforms.

The Town Hall Gardens c1950 C201013
The Town Hall's east front can be seen through the trees; the
lowest part of the gardens, in the former railway cutting, is
to the right. The buildings on the left, the old police station,
were demolished in 1980 and the park was subsequently
enlarged and re-opened by the Queen on 21 June 1983. In
honour of this they were renamed Queen's Gardens.

The Parish Church c1955 C201048
The medieval church was almost completely destroyed in a disastrous fire in 1867. It was rebuilt by the great Victorian church architect George Gilbert Scott, all but the 15th-century west tower and south porch, which survived the fire. This view was taken from St John's Road, beyond the 1960s dual carriageway which demolished the houses on the right; from here the grand scale of the church can be appreciated. Its association with the medieval Archbishop's Palace nearby accounts for its size, for the archbishops paid for its construction and six were buried in it, including John Whitgift, whose superb monument survived the fire.

The Parish Church c1950 C201007
The foreground has been swallowed up by the approaches to the pedestrian subway and by the dual carriageway western town centre by-pass, so all now is less tranquil than this 1950s view. To the right is the former churchyard, since 1956 a garden of remembrance and memorial to World War II Croydonians. Beyond the graveyard are the surviving buildings of the Archbishop's Palace, now extended as part of the Old Palace School, who are currently building a new prep school in Tudor style on the corner of Old Palace Road and Church Road.

The Whitgift Hospital of the Holy Trinity c1955 C201034
At the junction of George Street, High Street, North End and Crown Hill is one of the town's most remarkable survivals and a quiet haven that turns its back on the bustling town. Founded by John Whitgift, Archbishop of Canterbury, in 1596, the Hospital provided almshouses for sixteen men and sixteen women in rooms grouped round a grass quadrangle which you can see by peering through the archway into North End, as did Frith's photographer.

Whitgift Middle School c1950 C201040
Just behind the frontages of North End beyond Burtons were
the gates into the Whitgift Middle School. Its large ecclesiastical-
style tower was the centrepiece of the west range, designed
by Blomfield in 1869. This was a Victorian revival of Whitgift's
grammar school which had first opened in 1600. The Grammar
School moved out in 1931 to new buildings at Haling Park in
South Croydon. Whitgift Middle School moved in and in 1954 was
renamed the Trinity School of John Whitgift to avoid confusion
with the main Whitgift School. The school moved out to Shirley
in 1965, its Victorian school buildings and twelve acres of playing
fields a prime development site in the town centre.

The Tree Walk, Whitgift Middle School c1955 C201064

St Peter's Church c1955 C201059

The Tree Walk, Whitgift Middle School c1955

The school was demolished in 1965, and the vast mall shopping centre was constructed, accompanied by tall office blocks, including the twenty-one storey Rothschild House. The complex was opened by the Duchess of Kent in 1970, and has been almost rebuilt in the 1980s and 1990s. It is a far cry from Blomfield's Tudor collegiate Gothic style, and to many a sad loss.

St Peter's Church c1955

The arrival of the London and Brighton Railway in 1841, later the London, Brighton and South Coast Railway, led to much development along the course of the line and up the valley sides. These suburbs, some based around older villages, were provided with many Victorian churches to minister to the new inhabitants. St Peter's was built to cater for the population that had grown up around South Croydon Station.

St Peter's Church c1955

Here, we see the church from the gateway from St Peter's Road. Sir George Gilbert Scott had successfully captured the character of a village church of the medieval Decorated Gothic style. Started in 1850, it is quite early in his career, but had to be substantially reconstructed in 1865 following a major fire, the year after the spire was completed. Yew bushes have now grown up to obscure this view.

Coombe Cliff Gardens c1955

On the ridge east of the railway, the grounds of Coombe Cliff, an Italianate villa of about 1860, are now a public park. The villa was built for the Hornimans, tea merchants and public benefactors, as the English Heritage plaque informs us. Frederick John, the son, founded the Horniman Museum in Forest Hill. Their gardens remain remarkably intact, and in this view near the Coombe Hill entrance the trees and paths are very attractive, although there are now fewer planting beds.

St Peter's Church c1955 C201056

Coombe Cliff Gardens c1955 C201032

Coombe Cliff Gardens c1950 C201031

The Hornimans' villa remains as the Coombe Cliff Centre, run by the Council as an adult education centre. This area beyond the gardens themselves is more open, and overlies municipal reservoirs built in 1851. The walled yards have been laid out as a medieval herb garden, trees obscure the Croydon view and tower blocks obscure the Town Hall's tower. Behind the photographer is the old Norman style brick-built water tower of 1867. It was gutted in 1971, so you can no longer climb up for the spectacular views from its battlements.

Wandle Park c1950 C201055

This attractive park was laid out north of the railway line to Merton that curves away north-west from the West Croydon line to Epsom. Surrounded now by mature trees, its views of Croydon are obscured by the modern tramway viaduct. This view, looking towards Waddon New Road (new in the 1850s, that is), shows the bridge over the large pond that has since been completely filled in. The centre of the park is now flat grass, and, of course, the bridge has gone.

Wandle Park c1965 C201284
In 1955 the photographer would have had his feet in the water of the long-gone pond. He is looking towards town, with the tower of the parish church of St John at the end of Rectory Grove. The house on the right, No 96 Waddon New Road, remains, but the footbridge has moved 100 yards to the right, and the tram flyover masks most of the view.

Wandle Park c1955 C201057
This path originally circled the central large pond, which is, according to some, the source of the River Wandle as it starts its meander to the River Thames at Wandsworth. The pond has gone, and so have this path, railings, benches and flower beds: all is grass, although the grey metal cabinet behind the middle bench survives, now in isolation amid the grass.

The Old Town Centre

From South End to Broad Green via the Whitgift Hospital

High Street c1950 C201024
Our walk through the town starts at the junction where Lower Coombe Street and Coombe Road cross the High Street and South End, the road in which the photographer stands. In the distance, to get our bearings, is the corner tower of Millett's; the ball-finialled dome is that of the now-demolished Grand Theatre.

High Street c1955 C201052

A little further north and five years on from photograph No C201024, we look across the road by King's Parade, an Edwardian terrace of shops and flats, to the white rendered 1930s Collins building. Beyond, between it and the Grand Theatre, is the old Nalder and Collyer brewery, a site now occupied by the monstrous Leon House, a twenty-one storey tower block of 1969.

The Grand Theatre, High Street c1955 C201036

This closer view shows the Grand Theatre, now replaced by Grosvenor House, an office block which replaced it in 1960 and has since been refurbished in bilious pale green cladding. The theatre opened in 1896 and closed in 1959, and was originally known as the Grand Theatre and Opera House. Immediately to its left is the cupola of the Town Hall.

High Street c1960 C201151

In the middle distance the rounded corner building was replaced in about 1960 by the flyover which carries the A232 over the High Street. At the far right is the richly carved modillion eaves cornice and brickwork of Wrencote, a superb Queen Anne house; the sash-windowed house to its left, Wrencote House, is actually a scholarly and convincing neo-Georgian building of 1956 by Robert Cromie. The terrace beyond, with the Croydon Advertiser billboard, was replaced in the 1980s by the appalling Christopher Wren Yard, pallid and flat with a false mansard: an insult to Wrencote and Wrencote House.

High Street c1955
C201090
This photograph was taken from below where the flyover was soon to be built; note the tarmac strips replacing the tram lines. On the left is Whitgift Parade, dated at the corner 1900, with Dutch gables. The cupola beyond belongs to what is now the Hogshead, built as a bank in 1909. On the right the Davis Theatre stands beyond the 1928 neo-Georgian corner building.

◄ **High Street c1950**
C201025
The route now nears the Millett's corner, with Surrey Street market to its left and the High Street climbing to the right, its curve emphasised by the tramlines. The Georgian buildings on the left survive, but the Green Dragon pub beyond made way in the 1960s for the ugly Green Dragon House, again a lower block fronting the street and eleven storeys behind.

High Street c1965 C201137

This view should be compared with photograph No C201090, as it shows the Davis Theatre demolished and replaced by Davis House of 1961, low shops backed by a tall office tower. An extraordinary hole in the street frontage results. The Davis Theatre, opened in 1928, was vast; it had over 3,700 seats, and was used mainly as a cinema but also for concerts. A plaque records that Sir Thomas Beecham conducted the first performance by the Royal Philharmonic Orchestra here in 1946.

▼ The Greyhound c1955
C201075

The Greyhound has a late Victorian facade, which concealed an older Tudor and Georgian coaching inn. The restaurant's fascia dates from the 1930s, but was replaced in the early 1960s by St George's Walk shopping precinct and office blocks. On the left is the 1890s facade of Grant's department store, and at the brow of the hill is the Tudor brickwork of the Whitgift Hospital and Allders store beyond.

◄ North End c1955
C201085

The Whitgift Hospital of 1596 to 1599 occupies a key site in the townscape at the junction of George Street, High Street, Crown Hill and North End. It has four ranges that surround a tranquil grassed quadrangle. In this view the brickwork rebuilt after World War II bomb damage is clearly visible. The recently-opened tramway (1999) runs along George Street and Crown Hill in the foreground of this view.

Surrey Street, The Market c1965 C201145
Surrey House, on the left, and the Meat Market beyond, replaced the former gaol, while the street market continues to thrive. Near the telephone box a plaque commemorates the widening of the High Street under Mayor Edridge in 1896, the date of the Millett's corner tower. The Croydon Improvement Act of 1890 cleared away the slums of the market area as well as providing for the road widening.

◄ **Katharine Street c1955**
C201044
Since this view was taken, the north side of Katharine Street has been entirely rebuilt as the south side of the St George's Walk complex of the early 1960s. The Dutch gables of 1896 at the end belong to the High Street widening era, but nowadays the vista is dominated by BT's Rylands House beyond, a fifteen-storey block with the six-storey Surrey Road multi-storey car park beside it. The Town Hall side is virtually unchanged.

Surrey Street c1955 C201094
The medieval market place was a large triangular open space bounded by Surrey Street, High Street and Crown Hill. Classic market place encroachment took place over the years; stalls became permanent buildings. By the Victorian period, this area had become a slum with a warren of squalid lanes. On the left is the former gaol built in 1803; it was later converted to a warehouse and shop before being demolished in the 1950s.

George Street c1965 C201198
The western part of George Street survives considerably better than the eastern part beyond Park Lane. The new tramway runs along the left-hand side of the street in this view, which looks west to the start of Crown Hill beyond the gable and chimneys of the Whitgift Hospital. This Tudor building is surrounded and dwarfed by Victorian and later buildings, including Allder's fine 1897 Italianate white terracotta-faced building to the left of the 'Birthday' banner.

George Street c1955 C201043
East of the underpass on Park Lane, George Street is unrecognisable now. The Public Halls on the left with their channelled stucco ground floors have gone, as has Thrifts clock tower and warehouse. Immediately beyond, Nos 71 to 79 do remain, brick with buff terracotta dressings, as does a small villa of about 1830, the office of Shakespeare, the funeral directors, which was then dominated by the towering Thrifts warehouse wall. Everything on the right went for 1960s road widening.

▼ George Street c1965 C201199

Here the photographer looks east towards the underpass, past Jubilee Buildings of 1897 with their stone balconies. Beyond the traffic lights, only the building on the left with the white gable and the chimney stacks survives, Nos 71 to 79; even the modern office block has since been rebuilt.

▼ Crown Hill c1955 C201077

The walk now descends Crown Hill, down which the new trams run. On the left is the British Home Stores of 1929; beyond is a 1930s 'ocean liner'-style block with long steel windows and a keeled centre bay, complete with flagpole. The shoe repairers has been rebuilt in a rough replica, and is on the corner of Surrey Street. At the top of the hill is one of the gables of the Whitgift Hospital.

▲ Church Street c1965
C201154
From further downhill, in Church Street, we can see that the 1929 British Home Stores has been replaced by an up-to-the-minute mid 1950s sub-Festival of Britain building: all projecting frames and panels. To the left is virtually a teaching collection of the worst cheap urban architecture that the mean 1950s and 1960s could produce.

◀ **Crown Hill c1965** C201155
Back up Crown Hill, the lane
behind the benches is the
entrance to Middle Street,
which bisects the triangle
of the former market place;
the next junction on the
left is Surrey Street, the
original west boundary
of the market place. On
the right are the further
1950s bays of British Home
Stores, while the shops and
building behind on the right
have been replaced.

▼ **Church Street c1965** C201201

Church Street, one of the older town streets, curves towards the church; its tower and pinnacles can be seen beyond the row of mid-Georgian houses with painted brick, sash windows, heavy brick cornices, parapet and dormer windows. The building with the clock, a later Victorian frontage, has been replaced by the dire Argos building, but most of the other buildings in this view are intact.

▼ **North End c1955** C201039

North End runs north from the Whitgift Hospital road junction, and the first stretch used to be dominated by the two department stores, Kennards and Allders. The former, on the left, noted for its zoo, was recently demolished to be replaced by The Drummond Centre, a shopping centre and a Debenhams store. Allders, on the right, has a long stone facade with occasional columns and incised piers. This dates from around 1926; it would not be out of place in London's Regent Street.

▲ **North End c1965** C201203

Broadly speaking, most of the pre-1850 houses and shops on North End were rebuilt in the late 19th century, and some have been rebuilt again since. The modern Drummond Centre replaced the west side as far as Batchelors. The quirky gabled building with the clock survives, built in an ornate almost Swiss chalet style. Much of North End is now partly pedestrianised, and herringbone paviours stretch as far as the eye can see.

◄ **North End c1965** C201112
Further north along the west
side, Weaver to Wearer,
with its 1960 panels, is
much improved now that
the 1960s panels have
been removed to expose
good ornate first floor oriel
windows. It is now a Burger
King restaurant. The tower
on the left survives, but it
has lost the cupola seen in
photograph No C201203;
the Empire Theatre's dome
and cupola surmounted by
Hermes also gave way to
progress, and their site now
provides an access into the
Whitgift Centre.

North End c1950

C201018

This view looks back south towards the Town Hall tower, which forms a superb close to the vista. The buildings on the far left have been demolished. The Odeon Cinema beyond, showing 'Miranda' starring Glynis Johns, survives, but as a poor shadow with the facade scraped flat and mosaic-tiled: the 1960s have done their worst again. The grand late Victorian buildings beyond with corner turrets are unchanged, and the Arabic dome to Prince's on the right survives.

North End c1950

C201015

The new trams that started running in 1999 represent a revival of the system that ran from Edwardian times until the last tram ran in 1951. They were powered by overhead electric wires carried on elegant standards, or, as here, on cables attached to buildings on each side of the road.

◄ **North End c1960** C201076
This view looks north. Horne's men's clothes shop is in a building dated 1910, which fortunately survives. It is in an unusual late Arts and Crafts style; it is worthy of careful examination, for its judicious use of stone, decoration and design elements combine to produce an austere but highly creative version of Tudor architecture. To the right was the entrance to Whitgift School, but it is now an entrance to the Whitgift Shopping Centre.

◄ North End c1965 C201205
To the left of the long 1920s stone facade of Allders, the 1930s Tudor-style buildings are in brick with stone dressings; W H Smith's in the centre has coats of arms in the panels under the windows. Allders is celebrating its 104th birthday, so the view can be dated to 1966 - Joshua Allder opened his first shop in North End in 1862.

▼ North End c1965 C201204
Hornes, the fine 1910 building at the far right, survives, but the long row of gabled shops and flats has been demolished and rebuilt. The replacement is a distinctly less satisfying visual experience. By 1965 the Empire Theatre, its cupola crowned by a statue of Hermes, next to the tall brick building in the middle distance on the right with the gables and turret, has been demolished.

◄ North End c1955 C201078
Further north, and approaching West Croydon, we reach a further good example of 1930s commercial building. Marks and Spencer adopts a pared-down classical style for its stone facade, while the building beyond with continuous windows is more 'Moderne'. Marks and Spencer have, since this view was taken, expanded into this building. The partial pedestrianisation ends just near it.

London Road c1960
C201123
The mid-Victorian
expansion of Croydon
reached far along
the road to London,
encouraged here by the
arrival of the railway; it
passed beneath North
End on its route from
Norwood Junction,
where it leaves the
London to Brighton
line to Epsom. The Old
Fox and Hounds pub
on the left has a more
rural character with its
ornate bargeboards in
the gables, and deeper
eaves than the terraces
to its north with their
regular parapets and
grids of windows.

West Croydon c1950 C201019

In the 1920s and 1930s, the area around West Croydon Station and the cross-roads with Ruskin Road and Station Road, the A212, was redeveloped, and the railway station became a smart Southern Electric white Moderne building. At this time the trams still ran north of the junction heading for the London Road.

North End c1955 C201042

By 1950 the tram goes no further than the cross-roads. The station is in the building with the National Westminster Bank, while Woodhouse, in the curving corner building, has gone: it is now Maplins Electronics, but the building remains. The new trams now cross North End, running along Tamworth Road in the left foreground across to Station Road, roughly on the same line as the old tram wires in this view.

London Road c1950 C201027

A little north of West Croydon Station, the Victorian character of the road with its long terraces is little changed above shop-front level: there are two storeys above, usually two windows wide per unit, surmounted by a parapet above a cornice up to the 1860s, or with projecting eaves after 1870. On the left is West Croydon Methodist Church, a large building with a tower and spire. It has since been demolished, and the Methodists now meet in the architecturally mean former church hall at the back of the site.

◀ **London Road c1950** C201029
Further north, London Road passes through Broad Green, still with the tramway. The area was once quite smart, and the mid-Victorian villas on the left show this. The former United Reformed Church of 1866, with its tall and elegantly-proportioned spire, all built in Kentish ragstone, is now the Oshwal Hahajanwadi; to its immediate south is the 14-storey Phillips office block with the seven-storey Concord House beyond: the jam in a modern sandwich.

A Modern Town for the 1960s

The Flyover c1969 C201289
This view looks across the Croydon Flyover, a proud piece of highway engineering, towards the amazingly transformed skyline of Croydon as it emerged after the Croydon Corporation Act of 1956. No other town of comparable size embraced redevelopment with such enthusiasm, and in a mere decade all this was achieved: new modern roads, underpasses, overpasses, dual carriageways and above all immense numbers of high office blocks. Several more have been built since, including Ryland House to the left of the Flyover. You can just make out the previous tallest building: the Town Hall tower, now dwarfed.

▼ High Street 1968 C201183

The next two views show one of the new office developments under construction. The cliff of building is Leon House, eventually to reach 21 storeys. The view is taken from South End. While the buildings on the right survive, including the Georgian terrace at the right, the tall buildings on the left have been replaced by the 1980s answer to office design: gloomy brown brick with brown mortar and dark brown tinted glass, imaginatively named Nos 2-4 South End.

▼ High Street 1968 C201184

We are further north at the Coombe Road junction. Compare this view with the first in Chapter 2, C201024, taken in about 1948. The 1930s corner buildings are about to be overwhelmed visually. Leon House, designed by Tribich, Liefer and Starkin, is under construction, and there are a further nine storeys to go.

▲ Park Lane c1965 C201239

Along High Street the tower blocks are intermittent, but between this and East Croydon station there was almost total redevelopment: eastern George Street's buildings almost completely disappeared, and Park Lane and Wellesley Road became the focus for this new commercial centre. Here we look north along Park Lane towards the George Street cross-roads with the Fairfield Halls on the right.

◄ **The Underpass c1965**
C201170
This view looks south along Wellesley Road towards the underpass, with Norfolk House on the left; this was built in 1958 to 1959, and was in fact the first of the new office blocks to follow the 1956 Act. Nestle's tower is on the right behind the former Electricity Board offices, currently empty, a mere four storeys high and built in 1940. Beyond the underpass can be seen the side elevation of the Fairfield Halls.

The Underpass c1965

C201208

Taken from the Fairfield Halls roof, this view shows the underpass which carries the north-south route under George Street. The old town intrudes in the middle ground on the left, and a crane works on the Whitgift Centre beyond. On the left is the very tall St George's House, now Nestle's offices; built in 1962 to 1964, it towers twenty-four storeys, with the frames clad in Portland stone panels.

◄ **St Matthew's Church c1965** C201249
Immediately east of Suffolk House was St Matthew's parish church, designed by Blomfield and built in 1866. In 1965 it survives, a forlorn piece of the past amid the brave new world of Croydon. It lost its churchyard to the dual carriageway; then, with few people living in the centre, it was eventually closed and demolished. It is commemorated in the name of the 1980s seven-storey tower in dark brown brick and brown-tinted glass, St Matthew's House.

Suffolk House c1965
C201193

Suffolk House on the right is one of the earlier blocks of 'New Croydon'. It has four ranges surrounding a lightwell and angled corners. Designed by Raglan Squire and completed in 1961, it has the classic early 1960s coloured panel below a window style. George Street was widened into a dual carriageway at the same time, and both the office blocks beyond have since been rebuilt.

The Church c1965
C201127

This view shows the church isolated amid pavings, bereft of a churchyard setting, although a church hall was built in 1961 with a then-modish steep high gable and grid glazing. The office tower behind was replaced in the 1990s by Mondial House, and the mid 19th-century terrace on the other side of George Street was replaced by a ten-storey tower, Amp House.

Suffolk House and the Fairfield Halls c1965
C201167

Seen from the north-west corner of George Street as we look across the traffic island above the underpass, the 1960s buildings look distinguished and clean-lined, and one can see why they were then admired. Suffolk House nowadays looks dated, but Croydon College and the Fairfield Halls beyond have stood the test of time well.

The Denning Hall c1965 C201143
The building was designed by Robert Atkinson and built as Croydon Technical College between 1953 and 1959.
This is the elevation facing College Road, parallel to George Street. It is now Croydon College, and its entrance is
concealed by a two-bay canopy; the best elevation is that to Park Lane, seen in views C201167 and C201208, with
its two side wings with sculptures of Vulcan and Minerva.

The Fairfield Halls c1965 C201211
Also by Robert Atkinson and Partners, the Fairfield Halls were opened in 1962 and have proved a great success:
I remember going to numerous concerts there in the mid 1960s from my home in Carshalton when the
building was new and exciting, a positive rival to the Royal Festival Hall. This view illustrates the eclectic mix of
entertainment on offer.

The Town Hall Gardens and The Fairfield Halls c1965 C201240
A deceptively rural setting is provided by a view from Queen's Gardens, with the dual carriageway out of sight behind the railings (which have now gone). The Fairfield Halls is always referred to in the plural, for beside the concert hall there is the Arnhem Gallery to the right and the Ashcroft Theatre to the left. A black and white view does no justice to the lilac mosaic panels the designers used.

The Law Courts c1970 C201250
Behind the Fairfield Halls and fronting Barclay Road are the Law Courts, yet another building by Robert Atkinson and Partners; it was slightly later, being completed in 1969. The courtrooms are extruded on either side of the central entrance block, and there is extensive use of polished granite cladding, but the building is not considered as successful in architectural terms as is the Fairfield Halls or Croydon College.

The New Shopping Centre c1970 C201270

This is an interior view of phase one of the Whitgift Shopping Centre, which now occupies most of the land behind North End and Wellesley Road, the site of Whitgift School and its playing fields. At the time, the covered shopping mall was a new concept in England, and its opening in October 1970 by the Duchess of Kent caused great excitement. From 1986 a major rebuilding and alteration programme swept away and modernised the whole complex: the 1970 view somehow looks rather quaint and from a different era.

The Parish Church Hall c1965 C201261

The last view in this section shows new building mania reach the edge of the old town with a new church hall for the medieval parish church of St John - it is in the rather good style of the time for such buildings. The hall, by Graham and Denis Crump, was opened by the Archbishop of Canterbury in January 1960, the thousandth anniversary of the parish of Croydon, just as a brave new world of tower blocks swept in to transform the ancient town.

A Short Circuit Around Croydon

**Shirley,
St John's Parish Church c1955** S556021

Our tour starts in Shirley and Addiscombe to the east of Croydon. St John's parish church of 1856 is, like St Peter's, South Croydon, by Sir George Gilbert Scott. The lych gate, now ivy-less, and the iron kissing gate on the left, survive. In the churchyard is a monument to John Ruskin's father, John James, who died in 1864, and his mother who died in 1871.

Shirley, The Windmill c1965 S556064
This windmill now sits just off the Upper Shirley Road amid a close of executive houses, Post Mill Close, which recently replaced the 1960s school seen in this view. The mill was built in 1854 and ceased working in 1892. It replaced a timber one of 1808 and is a tower mill in tarred brick. Owned by Croydon Council, it is open for guided tours on some summer Sunday afternoons.

Addiscombe, Shirley Hills Road c1965 A267015
A little south of the windmill, this view shows some of the earlier housing before suburbia swept through Shirley. This is actually Upper Shirley, over a hundred metres above sea level, at the junction with Oaks Road, still separated from Shirley proper. The stucco houses date from around 1840. The timber building on the left has gone, to be replaced by a close of mock-Tudor houses.

Shirley, Oaks Road c1955 S556016

Shirley
Oaks Road c1955
Oaks Road runs south-west between a farm and golf course behind the houses on the right and the well-wooded Addington Hills on the left. This view looks south-west past Timber Cottage, whose white gable is prominent on the right. The far end of the road, just before its junction, is now crossed by the new tramway on its way to Addington.

Shirley
The Hills c1960
This view is actually in the Addington Hills, a popular location for dog walking, running, jogging and just walking or picnicking. These pebbly and sandy hills climb about a hundred feet from the Oaks Road to a peak of 433 feet above sea level. West of the former tea-room there is a walled platform view point; it was installed in 1960 to commemorate Croydon's millenary by Lt Col Basil Monk - there are indeed fine views across Croydon from here.

Shirley, The Hills c1960 S556031

Shirley, The Tea House c1960 S556034
The Tea House is well remembered by those who grew up in Croydon in the 1950s as a place where they could get ice creams as well as tea. It was built in the 1930s, and is now the Royal Garden Chinese Restaurant. The glazed tea room has been replaced by a modern plastic Victorian-style conservatory. Nearby there is the start of a Trim Trail, a now-popular fad in which various exercise stations are located so that keen types can jog between them, do a dozen chin-ups or whatever and jog to the next point.

Addiscombe, Coombe Woods c1965 A267014
These pebbly and sandy hills support tall pine trees and silver birches, and there is a great deal of bracken and some heather; other trees include oaks and sycamores. The car parks are well used. The Addington and Shirley hills stretch for over three miles; the centre part is occupied by two golf courses where sandy, quick draining pebbly soils and pine trees suit the golf course designer well.

Addiscombe, Shirley Road, The Parade c1965 A267010
In the 1920s and 1930s, Croydon's suburbs moved eastwards along the foot of the Addington and Shirley Hills, with estates and new housing engulfing earlier hamlets and the sparser and more isolated Victorian and Edwardian colonisation of Shirley. The hills kept the new developments from merging with the village of Addington, and the grounds of Addington Place were conserved as golf courses.

Shirley, Shirley Road c1955 S556002
The Parade, built at the junction of Shirley Road and Addiscombe Road in 1927, epitomises the inter-war affection for past architectural styles; it was felt that they gave an identity and character to the suburbs, which could all too easily be amorphous. Here the Tudor style was chosen: half timbering, tile-hung gables, oriel windows and leaded light casements.

Shirley, Shirley Road c1955 S556006
This is another view of the Parade in Shirley, this time with an Austin Seven parked outside, still a common sight in the 1950s. On the other side of Shirley Road, south of this viewpoint, are the buildings of the Trinity School. This name had been given to the Whitgift Middle School, which had been on its site behind North End in the centre of Croydon from 1931 to 1964 before moving to these new buildings set in generous grounds north of Shirley Park Golf Course.

Shirley, Hartland Way c1955 S556010
No suburb was complete without a public library: here we see Shirley's 1930s one with a sun and its rays over the entrance door, a typical 1920s and 1930s design motif. Since this view was taken, the parapets to the hipped-roofed section have been removed and eaves formed - a shame, but at least the building survives and is still in use as a library.

Shirley, All Saint's Church, Spring Park c1960 S556042
Spring Park was laid out between the two World Wars and after. In this view, the Church of All Saints on Brindle Avenue is at the corner of what is still an undeveloped road, now Farm Drive. Soon after this view, the Drive was developed on land advertised in this view. The church is an interestingly-massed one in brick, with a very substantial tower and lower wings. Stone and oak window frames give it a Tudor character.

South Norwood, The Memorial c1965 S614004
Our route takes us north-west. This view, in the Woodside area of South Norwood, is taken from Woodside Green, a large green that retains something of its rural character. There are a number of late Victorian villas, and even a few older houses pre-dating suburban expansion. This view looks towards the War Memorial, which supplanted a horse-trough in the 1920s.

Thornton Heath, London Road c1960

T262041

This view, east of the pond seen in photograph No T262023, whose railings can be seen on the left, shows the mix of building ages here, from mid-Victorian in the Plough and Harrow pub to Limes Parade of 1924, the three-storey parade of shops with flats over them on the right. In the middle distance is Thornton Heath's own version of the Crystal Palace tower.

▼ **Thornton Heath, The Pond c1955** T262023

Moving north-west, the brief itinerary reaches Thornton Heath, a Victorian development that eventually merged with Norwood, Norbury and Croydon. Here at the junction of Thornton Road and the London Road a large traffic island-cum-public open space has a pond and fountain round which buses, lorries and cars roar. Since this view was taken, the pond has been filled in and paved over, but many of the buildings survive, including the gabled one with Gothic arched windows of 1887, now a Post Office.

▼ **Thornton Heath, The Station c1955** T262018

Much of the suburb owed its development to the railway. The station booking hall, a competent design built on the bridge over the railway, dates from about 1900, and was erected for the London, Brighton and South Coast Railway. The line now serves the Connex Metro. The canopy and cupola have gone, while the South Suburban Co-op is now a florist's shop.

▲ **Thornton Heath, The Clock Tower and Parchmore Road c1947**

T262017

This late Victorian clocktower is just east of the station, at the junction of Brigstock Road, High Street and Parchmore Road. It is unchanged, although much has changed around it, including the loss of most of the trees and a redesign of the island beyond. To the left, out of the picture, is a Tesco supermarket, while the houses seen behind the clocktower do survive.

◄ **Beddington c1960** B50029
Moving west of Croydon we reach Beddington, a village of two halves, a green and open one north of Croydon Road and a suburban one to its south. Here the photographer looks north-east from the Plough Lane railway bridge across a sports field and suburban development. We can see the semis of Bristow Road and Croydon Power Station and the giant cooling towers: all gone except for the two tall chimneys, which are now part of an Ikea store. Trees obscure the view now, and the playing fields are in a sorry state.

◀ **Beddington,
The Broadway c1960**
B50014
Round the corner on
Croydon Road, The
Broadway assumes a
different architectural
character with much use of
red brick horizontal bands,
soldier courses and simple
pilasters, all in contrast to
the plum brick of the main
body of the walls.

Beddington, The Broadway c1960

B50028

Further north along Plough Lane, where it meets Croydon Road, is the Plough pub, a late 19th-century building of some quality, which forms an island with a road to its west and east. To the right is The Broadway, a three storey 1950s development with shops on the ground floor and a library in the centre: it is still a library today.

Beddington, The Church c1960

B50035

North of Croydon Road the great hall of the old manor house of the Carew family survives, alongside the parish church, whose west tower was built by the Carews. The manor, now Carew Manor School, was extensively altered and rebuilt; it assumed its present form in the 1860s when it was converted for the Lambeth Female Orphan Asylum. The central clocktower can be seen in this view behind the gables to the left of the church tower.

Beddington, The Grange c1960 B50004

Carew Manor and the church face Beddington Park, the grounds of the manor; they were re-landscaped in the later 19th century, and comprise the southern part of undeveloped land that stretches to Mitcham Common from the north side of Croydon Road, and includes the Hackbridge Sewage Farm. The Grange and its gardens, accessed from London Road, were at the west end and long incorporated into Beddington Park.

Wallington, The Grange Park c1955 W11054
The Grange was a rather good Tudor-style building of 1879 with timber-framing to the upper floor, a stone and flint ground floor and picturesque clusters of chimneys. Unfortunately, it burnt down in 1960 and was replaced by a pallid pastiche in 1967; it has since been refurbished and has even less personality. The pond and its surrounding walls, pergolas and footbridge at the left all survive, as does its former gardens to the north of the boating lake.

Wallington, The Green c1965 W11152
Wallington, to the west of Beddington, has its oldest houses around The Green, where Manor Road meets Acre Lane or the Croydon Road. Several Regency stucco houses survive here, and a few earlier ones a little north along London Road by the River Wandle. We are looking south-east across The Green; the trees have now been replaced. The mid 19th-century building on the right is the Duke's Head pub, now with a large matching hotel wing added.

Wallington
Manor Road c1955 W11033
This view looks south along Manor Road. The Duke's Head and The Green are on the right,
and 1880s shops and flats are on the left; the far left one is now replaced by a 1980s office
block, Green View House. In the distance is the spire of Holy Trinity parish church of 1867,
built of flint and stone, in which I was confirmed in 1965.

Wallington, Manor Road c1955 W11028
The railway arrived in 1847 and led to much expansion further south down Manor Road. Here we look back from beside the station towards Holy Trinity's spire. The pub, the stucco building on the right, survives as O'Neills, as do the 1860s and 1880s buildings on the left, but the station has been rebuilt as an office block with station below; the greenery and trees on the left disappeared in the 1980s under a six-storey brown brick and brown glass office block, Carew House.

Wallington, Woodcote Road c1960 W11080
We are looking south from the railway bridge, where Woodcote Road continues as Manor Road southwards. The long Edwardian terrace on the left climbs the hill well: its bay windows give a strong rhythm, and the corner with Ross Parade is emphasised by a Dutch gable. The bank on the right, competent 1920s neo-Georgian, has been replaced by a modern pub. In the distance is the spire of the United Reformed Church.

Wallington
Woodcote Road c1955
W11007

Most Saturday mornings in the early 1960s my brother and I would come shopping here from our house in Carshalton, often on our way to a stamp collectors' shop in Stafford Road. The shops on the left were built at different times from the 1920s to the 1950s, and never achieved the unity of the right-hand side. The view is now closed by the six-storey offices of Canon just beyond the railway bridge.

Wallington, Christchurch c1965 W11083
Drastic change has taken place here since this view was taken. The United Reformed Church of 1887, with its red brick and stone dressings, has gone to make way for a Sainsbury's supermarket and decked parking. The shops on the right went, as did the nearer shops down the hill, for a 1960s wind-blown shopping precinct that never prospered much. The church hall to the left was the scene of many dances and events, as I recall from my teenage years in the mid 1960s.

Wallington, Town Hall c1965 W11141
The Town Hall and Library survive, facing each other across a garden and pond. The Town Hall, whose other facade faces Woodcote Road, is a distinguished building of 1935. The right wing contains the local driving test centre; here I passed first my motorcycle and then my car driving tests. The library followed in 1936, and now has a coffee shop to entice readers in. Both are by Robert Atkinson, and are good examples of their kind for the suburbs.

Index

FRITH PRODUCTS & SERVICES

Francis Frith would doubtless be pleased to know that the pioneering publishing venture he started in 1860 still continues today. Over a hundred and forty years later, The Francis Frith Collection continues in the same innovative tradition and is now one of the foremost publishers of vintage photographs in the world. Some of the current activities include:

INTERIOR DECORATION

Today Frith's photographs can be seen framed and as giant wall murals in thousands of pubs, restaurants, hotels, banks, retail stores and other public buildings throughout the country. In every case they enhance the unique local atmosphere of the places they depict and provide reminders of gentler days in an increasingly busy and frenetic world.

PRODUCT PROMOTIONS

Frith products are used by many major companies to promote the sales of their own products or to reinforce their own history and heritage. Frith promotions have been used by Hovis bread, Courage beers, Scots Porage Oats, Colman's mustard, Cadbury's foods, Mellow Birds coffee, Dunhill pipe tobacco, Guinness, and Bulmer's Cider.

GENEALOGY AND FAMILY HISTORY

As the interest in family history and roots grows world-wide, more and more people are turning to Frith's photographs of Great Britain for images of the towns, villages and streets where their ancestors lived; and, of course, photographs of the churches and chapels where their ancestors were christened, married and buried are an essential part of every genealogy tree and family album.

FRITH PRODUCTS

All Frith photographs are available Framed or just as Mounted Prints and Posters (size 23 x 16 inches). These may be ordered from the address below. Other products available are- Address Books, Calendars, Jigsaws, Canvas Prints, Notelets and local and prestige books.

THE INTERNET

Already ninety thousand Frith photographs can be viewed and purchased on the internet through the Frith websites and a myriad of partner sites.

For more detailed information on Frith companies and products, look at this site:
www.francisfrith.com

See the complete list of Frith Books at: www.francisfrith.com
This web site is regularly updated with the latest list of publications from The Francis Frith Collection. If you wish to buy books relating to another part of the country that your local bookshop does not stock, you may purchase on-line.

For further information, trade, or author enquiries please contact us at the address below:
The Francis Frith Collection, Unit 6, Oakley Business Park, Wylye Road, Dinton, Wiltshire SP3 5EU.
Tel: +44 (0)1722 716 376 Fax: +44 (0)1722 716 881 Email: sales@francisfrith.co.uk

See Frith products on the internet at www.francisfrith.com

FREE PRINT OF YOUR CHOICE

Mounted Print
Overall size 14 x 11 inches (355 x 280mm)

Choose any Frith photograph in this book.
Simply complete the Voucher opposite and return it with your remittance for £3.50 (to cover postage and handling) and we will print the photograph of your choice in SEPIA (size 11 x 8 inches) and supply it in a cream mount with a burgundy rule line (overall size 14 x 11 inches). **Please note**: aerial photographs and photographs with a reference number starting with a "Z" are not Frith photographs and cannot be supplied under this offer. Offer valid for delivery to one UK address only.

PLUS: Order additional Mounted Prints at HALF PRICE - £9.50 each (normally £19.00)
If you would like to order more Frith prints from this book, possibly as gifts for friends and family, you can buy them at half price (with no additional postage and handling costs).

PLUS: Have your Mounted Prints framed
For an extra £18.00 per print you can have your mounted print(s) framed in an elegant polished wood and gilt moulding, overall size 16 x 13 inches (no additional postage and handling required).

IMPORTANT!

These special prices are only available if you use this form to order. You must use the ORIGINAL VOUCHER on this page (no copies permitted). We can only despatch to one UK address. This offer cannot be combined with any other offer.

Send completed Voucher form to:
The Francis Frith Collection, Unit 6, Oakley Business Park, Wylye Road, Dinton, Wiltshire SP3 5EU

CHOOSE A PHOTOGRAPH FROM THIS BOOK

Voucher for **FREE** and Reduced Price Frith Prints

Please do not photocopy this voucher. Only the original is valid, so please fill it in, cut it out and return it to us with your order.

Picture ref no	Page no	Qty	Mounted @ £9.50	Framed + £18.00	Total Cost £
		1	Free of charge*	£	£
			£9.50	£	£
			£9.50	£	£
			£9.50	£	£
			£9.50	£	£
			£9.50	£	£

Please allow 28 days for delivery.
Offer available to one UK address only

* Post & handling	£3.50
Total Order Cost	£

Title of this book . . . .

I enclose a cheque/postal order for £ . . . .
made payable to 'The Francis Frith Collection'

OR please debit my Mastercard / Visa / Maestro card, details below

Card Number:

Issue No (Maestro only):   Valid from (Maestro):

Card Security Number: Expires:

Signature:

Name Mr/Mrs/Ms . . . .

Address . . . .

. . . .

. . . .

. . . . Postcode . . . .

Daytime Tel No . . . .

Email . . . .

Valid to 31/12/12

Can you help us with information about any of the Frith photographs in this book?

We are gradually compiling an historical record for each of the photographs in the Frith archive. It is always fascinating to find out the names of the people shown in the pictures, as well as insights into the shops, buildings and other features depicted.

If you recognize anyone in the photographs in this book, or if you have information not already included in the author's caption, do let us know. We would love to hear from you, and will try to publish it in future books or articles.

An Invitation from The Francis Frith Collection to Share Your Memories

The 'Share Your Memories' feature of our website allows members of the public to add personal memories relating to the places featured in our photographs, or comment on others already added. Seeing a place from your past can rekindle forgotten or long held memories. Why not visit the website, find photographs of places you know well and add YOUR story for others to read and enjoy? We would love to hear from you!

www.francisfrith.com/memories

Our production team

Frith books are produced by a small dedicated team at offices near Salisbury. Most have worked with the Frith Collection for many years. All have in common one quality: they have a passion for the Frith Collection.

Frith Books and Gifts

We have a wide range of books and gifts available on our website utilising our photographic archive, many of which can be individually personalised.

www.francisfrith.com

Free Print – see overleaf